MW01043128

TABLE OF

INTRO

Sometimes it can be easy to think of God as a best friend who's moved away. You relate to each other from a distance, if at all. In fact, He probably has other, more important things to do and other people to care about rather than you. After all, you're just an average person; there are a lot more important things going on in the world.

Wow. Cue the sad instrumental music. That paragraph sounds pretty depressing. Good thing that God doesn't work that way. That means we shouldn't think that way either. While we must remember that we're not the center of God's universe, we can really get excited about the fact that God chose us and wants to have a relationship with us. Not like a relationship where you hang out at the mall together but a relationship with the Creator of the universe who gives us purpose and meaning in life. Wow! Now that deserves an excited scream that would rival the cheers of a winning touchdown!

Linked is all about God's relationship with His people—the way that His holy and just character seeks His people and makes a way for them to relate to Him. In response to Him, His people live in a way that shows His character to the world so that all people may come to worship Him with their lives.

So what does *Linked* have to do with you? Well, everything. Each devotion in this book talks about a part of God's story with His people. You are God's people, or one of God's people. As you read through each devotion, remember that you're part of the story of God's people. You relate to Him and others as a child of God. You're forever *Linked* to Him.

One of His,

Jenny Riddle
Writer & Editor

HOW TO USE *31: Linked. . .*

Now that you own this incredible little book, you may be wondering, "What do I do with it?"

Glad you asked. The great thing about this book is that you can use it just about any way you want.

It's not a system. It's a resource that can be used in ways that are as unique and varied as you are.

A few suggestions . . .

THE ONE-MONTH PLAN
On this plan, you'll read one devotion each day for a month. This is a great way to immerse yourself in the Bible for a month-long period. (OK, we realize that every month doesn't have 31 days. But 28 or 30 is close enough to 31, right?) The idea is to cover a lot of information in a short amount of time.

THE SCRIPTURE MEMORY PLAN
The idea behind this plan is to memorize the verse for each day's devotion; you don't move on to the next devotion until you've memorized the Scripture you're on. If you're like most people, this might take you more than one day per devotion. So this plan takes a slower approach.

THE "I'M NO WILLIAM SHAKESPEARE" PLAN
Don't like to write or journal? This plan is for you. . . . Listen, not everyone expresses themselves the same way. If you don't like to express yourself through writing, that's OK. Simply read the devotion for each verse, and then read the questions. Think about them. Pray through them. But don't feel as if you have to journal if you don't want to.

THE STRENGTH IN NUMBERS PLAN
God designed humans for interaction. We're social creatures. How cool would it be if you could go through *31: Linked* with your friends? Get a group of friends together. Consider agreeing to read five verses each week and then meeting to talk about them.

Pretty simple, right? Choose a plan. Or make up your own. But get started, already. What are you waiting for?

VERSE ONE

THERE IS NO ONE HOLY LIKE THE LORD; THERE IS NO
ONE BESIDES YOU; THERE IS NO ROCK LIKE OUR GOD.

1 SAMUEL 2:2

In the movie *The Incredibles*, a bitter man engineered a set of tools to help him simulate superpowers. He even gave himself a super name—Syndrome. He spent his life designing a machine that superheroes could not beat—only his remote control could tame it. After setting the machine to wreak havoc on the local citizens, Syndrome pretended to come to the rescue, setting himself up as the hero. But the machine learned how to defeat him, and Syndrome lost his remote control. He was inadequate to battle it without his remote control. The family of the Incredibles and their superhero friend were the only ones who could defeat Syndrome's machine. Unlike Syndrome, they had real superpowers. They weren't pretenders.

In 1 Samuel 1, the author portrayed Hannah as a very godly woman. Even so, Hannah's prayers weren't answered in the way that she wanted. She prayed to have a son but lived year after year without God providing a child. Despite the long years, Hannah continued to pray, and she promised God that she would dedicate her son to Him. God provided a son, and Hannah fulfilled her promise. Read 1 Samuel 2:1-10. Hannah knew that God alone had provided her son, Samuel. She expressed her knowledge that God was the only holy One, the only Provider, and the only Judge. He alone was God.

God is not a pretend God. He's completely holy, a continual Provider, and a worthy Judge. Because He's the true God, He's the one who can judge sin. He's the standard of holiness, and His justice demands that we conform to Him. Therefore, He provides just consequences for our sin. When we seek to live to His standards, we reflect God's holiness and justice.

1. How do you sometimes live as if you think that God is just a pretend God?

2. Why is it easy to think of God as a God of love but forget that He's also a God of justice?

3. How does God's holiness affect the decisions that you make?

VERSE?

The LORD reigns forever; he has established his throne for judgment. He will judge the world in righteousness; he will govern the peoples with justice.

PSALM 9:7-8

What if you were asked to judge Olympic figure skating? Seriously. This sounds absurd, right? After all, you probably wouldn't know a Salchow jump if it were done on your head. A delayed axel sounds like something a mechanic fixes on your car. And you're almost guaranteed not to know the difference between a mazurka jump and a toe walley. All in all, you'd be a very poor figure skating judge. You simply aren't qualified.

Hold that thought as you read Psalm 9:7-10. The Psalms are an impressive collection of writings. They were written by a variety of people, but David wrote most of them; most people think he wrote 75 of them. The rest were written by some guys you know (Solomon, Moses, and Asaph) and some guys you probably don't (the sons of Korah). At least one or two psalms had authors that are unknown today. Regardless, the Psalms have been an amazing source of strength, encouragement, and knowledge of God for centuries of believers. This passage is no different.

Go back and read verses 7 and 8 with our ice skating introduction in mind. What theme do you see that's similar in both? The idea of a judge, right? One of God's many roles is that of a judge. The difference between you as an ice skating judge and God as Judge of the entire world is that He's perfectly qualified. He's perfectly just. Therefore, He alone is able to judge humanity for our sins.

The idea of God as Judge makes some of us freak out. But it shouldn't. Jesus already paid our penalty on the cross! God will pass judgment on the world, but if we believe in and follow Jesus, our sentence has already been served. No need to freak out!

REFLECT

1. How do you feel when you think about God as one who will "judge the world in righteousness"?

2. So, you believe that God is the only one perfectly capable of judging the world. Knowing that, why do you think it's important that someone hold evil people accountable for their actions? (Hint: Think about the alternative. No accountability!)

3. If you get a little uneasy about God as judge, it's OK. If you've submitted your life to Jesus' lordship, the work He did on the cross saves you from God's judgment. Write a prayer thanking Jesus for His sacrifice (and thanking God for having this plan in mind all along).

verseTHREE
You hear, O LORD, the desire of the afflicted; you encourage them, and you listen to their cry . . .

PSALM 10:17

It's pretty depressing to think about all that's wrong in the world. There's a whole lot of disease, not enough clean water, and too many people fixated on evil. And that's just on a global level. What about you and your own little world of personal problems? Your best friend's parents are splitting up. Your mom lost her job. Someone at school is spreading a vicious rumor about you. Life isn't always fair, and it can sometimes seem that the tide has turned against you.

Read Psalm 10:12-18. This psalm was written as a lament about a world that was affected by sin—where destructive events happened and people committed evil acts. The author noted that these wicked people claimed that God wouldn't call them to account. However, the author also praised God that evil doesn't go unnoticed by Him. No matter what happens on earth, the Lord is still sovereign King. His holy and righteous character desires for evil to be rightly judged. His loving character defends those who are wronged by injustice. The Lord despises injustice and will bring His judgment to those who commit it and allow it.

The hard truth is that all of today's depressing events can sometimes make believing in God difficult. As humans, we often fail to see God's big picture and how He's working behind the scenes. Not only is He sovereign, He's personal enough to hear us. Even though the world seems crazy and out of our control, we can trust Scripture when it says that God reigns over everything. In the midst of circumstances that we don't understand, we can trust that He's our Comforter and our Healer. We can cry out to Him and believe that He notices injustice and will act against it.

reflect

1. What are some examples of problems in the world that cause you to question God's character?

2. What's the greatest example of God's comfort that you have seen displayed?

3. Think back to a time when you felt your world was falling apart. Did you cry out to God? How did He remain faithful to the promise He gives in this passage of Scripture?

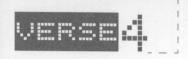

Defend the cause of the weak and
fatherless; maintain the rights of the
poor and oppressed.

PSALM 82:3

"I've successfully privatized world peace," boasted Tony Stark in *Iron Man 2*. Spiderman, a.k.a. Peter Parker, lived by more humble words: "With great power, comes great responsibility." Batman likewise kept a vigilant eye over Gotham City, maintaining peace and ensuring justice for those living under his watch. Superheroes are great. Something inside us naturally loves the idea of a hero saving the day. Though today's heroes and villains don't typically wear masks or makeup, justice is just as desperately needed in the real world as in movies and graphic novels.

Read Psalm 82:1-4. This psalm was written by Asaph, a praise leader during the time of King David. Imagine a courtroom setting where God was the ultimate Judge. In verse 1, the word *gods* meant influential people or human rulers who should have been using their positions of power to protect others. Instead, these so-called gods had been acting as criminals, corrupted by selfishness and favoritism. In verses 3 and 4, God ordered His people to rescue the oppressed. As God's representatives, they should have reflected His character by actively pursuing justice on behalf of those who were vulnerable.

The truth is that each of us falls into the courtroom drama. Like the oppressed, we all need rescuing—we can't save ourselves from sin and death. Christ saves us. Like the influential rulers, we now keep watch so as not to become hypocrites and villains—we don't want to know the truth of God's commands but live a lie. Finally, we're like the heroes. There are people all around us who need saving—people with spiritual, emotional, physical, material, and financial needs. There is no "privatization" of this great salvation for one person alone. In Christ we have great power and great responsibility. Go be a hero.

1. Describe a time when someone helped you do something that you couldn't have done on your own. How did you feel knowing someone was willing to help?

2. In what ways are you ignoring needs or even doing wrong to people around you? (Identify students who are lonely, awkward, picked on, disabled, bullied, poor, hurting, and so on. How are you showing them the love of Christ? If you're not, why not?)

3. Write a prayer asking God to open your eyes to indifference in your heart and injustice in others' lives. Pray for boldness to take action in changing those situations. Pray for a humble heart of compassion toward those in need.

YOUR EYES SAW MY UNFORMED BODY. ALL THE DAYS
ORDAINED FOR ME WERE WRITTEN IN YOUR BOOK
BEFORE ONE OF THEM CAME TO BE.
PSALM 139:16

Have you heard the saying, "It's not what you know; it's who you know"?
This statement is often true, whether you're looking for a part-time job or
trying out for a team. For example, if you're applying for a job and your
potential boss knows you, then he or she will be more likely to hire you
than a stranger. Your relationship with that person makes you valuable
to him or her. But, if you're a stranger, you're a name without a face and
story. The more you know and trust someone, the deeper the relationship
is.

Read Psalm 139:13-18. David wrote these verses as part of a poetic song.
He was an ordinary shepherd boy who became King of Israel. Throughout his life, David desired to live faithfully to God, the all-knowing One
described in this psalm. In David's description, God was not distant or
disinterested in him. God created David and knew him inside and out,
even before David was born. The phrase "knit together" meant he was
custom-designed by God. David described God's awesome knowledge to
show how intimately God cares for each of His people.

God's knowledge is far above ours, but He's not far from us. We're not
strangers to God. He created us, just as He did David, in order to have
a real relationship with us. Even before we were born, God completely
knew each of us. God has understood us, known us, and cared for us
from the beginning. We're valuable to Him. If we're there for those we
care about, how much more will God, our Creator, be there for us? The
One who made the heavens and the earth knit us together and desires a
relationship with us.

1. How does God's intimate knowledge of you shape the way you think of Him?

2. Think about how David described God. How would you describe God and your relationship with Him?

3. In what ways does the knowledge that you were created for a relationship with God affect the way you live?

VERSE 6

NOW IF YOU OBEY ME FULLY AND KEEP MY COVENANT, THEN OUT OF ALL NATIONS YOU WILL BE MY TREASURED POSSESSION.

EXODUS 19:5A

User agreements. Whether we're renewing our user agreements on iTunes, downloading videos, or installing software, these little user agreements consistently pop up. Basically, these agreements set user guidelines that we must follow in order to use the application, software, or video without violating any laws or regulations. These guidelines give us knowledge of how to use these items correctly.

Read Exodus 19:3-8. God led the Israelites out of Egypt about seven weeks before they came to Mt. Sinai. They'd already witnessed God's power as He miraculously rescued them from slavery. They also experienced God's care as He supernaturally provided food and water in the desert. The Israelites knew what God had done in their lives, but God wanted more than knowledge: He wanted to have a relationship with them. He made a covenant with them that outlined how this relationship could happen. Because God was holy, they could only interact with Him if they followed these guidelines. The Law was not meant to be a new kind of slavery for His people but a way for them to relate to Him on His holy terms.

Sometimes we can view the Bible as a series of rules that are supposed to tell us how to act as "good Christians." God's Word to us, however, should be taken in light of our relationship with Him. He doesn't want us to just be good people. He wants us to be His people who reflect His holiness to the world through our relationship with Him. His Word is a gift to us. If we accept it and spend time studying it, we know how to have this kind of relationship with Him. Even more important than a user agreement, God's Word guides us to know how to live so that we reflect Him.

REFLECT

1. How would you describe the Bible? How is that description different from thinking of God's Word as a gift to tell you how to have a relationship with Him?

2. How does spending time in God's Word help you to reflect Him to the world?

3. How does your life reflect the importance of God's Word to you?

verse SEVEN

And by that will, we have been made holy through the sacrifice of the body of Jesus Christ once for all.

HEBREWS 10:10

Near the end of 2009 a historic cold spell gripped most of the United States. The cold weather was still wreaking havoc across the South when 2010 rolled around. The Southeast experienced record lows. The residents of many cities were seriously unprepared.

Memphis was one of those cities. Faced with the reality of many Memphis residents being unequipped to handle the arctic weather, Memphis mayor A.C. Wharton did something remarkable. He brokered an agreement between the county, city, and Memphis Light, Gas and Water to turn the power back on for hundreds of people who had lost power because they'd failed to pay their bills. In doing so, Wharton likely saved lives. Jacqueline Mosley was one of those people. "I never thought that this would happen to me with the bill that I have, and no way to pay it," she said.

Read Hebrews 10:5-10. Hebrews was written mainly to a Jewish audience. The author of Hebrews was making the case for Jesus as Messiah. (We really don't know who "the author" is. Regardless, it's an awesome book.) This particular passage was talking about the once-for-all nature of Jesus' sacrifice on the cross. No longer was it necessary to sacrifice animals to be cleansed from sin's guilt: Jesus became the ultimate sacrifice!

The mayor of Memphis did something that residents couldn't do for themselves. The nature of Jesus' sacrifice is similar—except about a billion times greater in scale! Jesus did something for us that we couldn't do for ourselves: He paid the price for our sins. We were made holy in God's eyes by Jesus' work on the cross. He paid a debt we could never, ever pay ourselves and ultimately saved our lives.

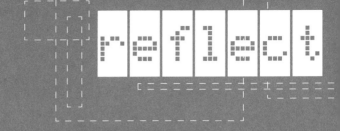

reflect

1. Think for a moment what you would do if you were standing before God. (Seriously, stop for a moment and picture it.) What are some of the things you would feel?

2. If you haven't already, think about how the sinfulness in your life would make you feel as you were standing before your perfectly good and righteous God. What thoughts come to mind?

3. Now remember that Jesus has made you holy! Remember that you can stand before God sinless because of Christ's sacrifice on the cross. Now how does that make you feel?

For we are God's workmanship, created in Christ Jesus to do good works, which God prepared in advance for us to do.

EPHESIANS 2:10

Remember the old Disney movie, *Pinocchio*? A lonely old man crafts a puppet that he hopes will turn into an actual human little boy. With the help of a blue fairy and a talking cricket dressed in a coat and tails, the puppet manages to get kidnapped, turned into a donkey, and then eaten by a whale. Finally, he becomes a real boy. Weird movie.

Take a look at Ephesians 2:10. Paul called believers *God's workmanship*. Paul recognized that God is the Creator of all people, but when people become Christ-followers by receiving God's grace through faith in Christ, they become new creations of God. This salvation is not random, and it isn't for the benefit of people's personal happiness. News flash: God graciously offers His salvation for His good purposes. Paul knew that God has a purpose for His people. He saves them and works in their lives so that they can accomplish the good works for which He created them.

We're not puppets carved by a delusional woodworker in 1920s Italy. We're complex human beings, created by an infinite God, to set the world on fire with our good works that are done in His name and for His glory. (Read that last sentence again and again until you get it.) Everything from telling our best friend about Christ to refusing to perpetuate a rumor—big things and small things—has a purpose. It's not arbitrary or an accident that we are who we are, when we are, and where we are. Geppetto made Pinocchio but only had hopes of what would come in Pinocchio's future (again, sort of crazy). God, the Creator of the universe, created us for a specific purpose and works intimately in our lives to carry out His purposes in our lives yesterday, today, and every day (not crazy).

1. How does knowing the purpose of your salvation change your perspective on why you were saved?

2. What is your reaction to reading that you are God's workmanship? How does that make you feel?

3. What are some examples of good works that you can do to carry out God's purpose in your life today? In the next year? In the next five years?

VERSE NINE

THE WRATH OF GOD IS BEING REVEALED FROM HEAVEN AGAINST ALL THE GODLESSNESS AND WICKEDNESS OF MEN WHO SUPPRESS THE TRUTH BY THEIR WICKEDNESS.
ROMANS 1:18

If we're honest, sometimes we live as if God were Santa Claus. He knows all about us and wants to make us happy if we behave. We like to focus on the mercy, love, and grace of God's character—you know, the stuff that makes us feel good inside. But the verses in the Bible about God's judgment and hatred of our sin don't really give us the warm fuzzies, do they?

Romans 1:18 is one of those verses. Go ahead; take a look at Romans 1:18-19. Sounds pretty grim, right? "The wrath of God"—could there be a more terrifying phrase? Paul made it clear that God is not happy with sin; it's a very serious matter to Him. He's angry about sin because it goes against His nature. Therefore, out of His holy character, God judges people for their sin. Paul said in verse 19 that God made His character plain to everyone so that they don't have an excuse to reject His holiness. That means that all people are under the judgment of God—no one is excused.

God is the majestic Creator of the universe. The holy One. He's good and merciful and graceful but most certainly not Santa Claus. He's not concerned with our happiness as much as with our holiness. His holiness demands our holiness. The good news is that Jesus Christ is in the picture. And because of His great sacrifice for us, He takes our place when God's wrath comes on us. Without Jesus, the full weight of God's wrath would be upon each of us. Let us live each day grateful to Christ for what He's done for us and be thankful that God loved us so much that He sent Him.

1. Why is it easy for you to forget that God's holiness requires His judgment in addition to His love and grace?

2. How did God show His mercy to you even when He was judging your sin?

3. How does this verse compel you to tell others about Christ?

> BECAUSE THE LORD DISCIPLINES THOSE HE
> LOVES, AS A FATHER THE SON HE DELIGHTS IN.
> ## PROVERBS 3:12

Elizabeth Lambert. Her unsportsmanlike conduct gained infamy overnight thanks to YouTube and ESPN. Throughout 2009's soccer conference matchup between Brigham Young University (BYU) and the University of New Mexico, the young athlete collided with, tripped, punched, and pulled the hair of her opponents. Lambert yanked one BYU player's ponytail with such force that the girl's head snapped backward as her body crumpled to the ground. What was obvious thanks to video replay went virtually unnoticed by referees during the game. Certainly a red card (meaning ejection from the game), not only would have been fair, but expected, right?

Read Proverbs 3:11-12. A proverb is a wise saying, coaching people in practical matters of godly life. Here, the writer used affectionate language to remind his audience that rules are in place for good reason. God is a loving Father who has established an order in life that is best for everyone. For people who violate the rules of conduct, the appropriate and loving thing to do is to discipline them. This discourages behavior that ruins life for everyone while it also encourages freedom to move within the boundaries that God has set. With this loving discipline, God's children will become more like Him.

If we're honest, sometimes we feel like God is unfair and likes to ruin our fun. Nothing could be further from the truth! Think about playing soccer without rules or boundaries. That would be unfair and chaotic. So why do we view life and God differently? Trust that the rules and boundaries He has set are for our benefit. When we do step out of bounds, either carelessly or intentionally, we should be good sports and accept His warnings. Any discipline we experience is not only fair, but to be expected. It's ultimately for our benefit to help us become more like Him.

REFLECT

1. Describe what life would be like without rules or consequences. It might sound fun at first, but really think through
what it would be like if people did whatever they wanted.

2. When was the last time you were disciplined (in home,
school, sports, and so on)? What did you do? What did you (or
should you) learn from the discipline?

3. Maybe you do or maybe you don't have a family example of godly
wisdom and loving discipline. Either way, your heavenly Father loves
you completely, no matter what your situation or what you may have
done. Pray that you will trust His guidance, heed His warnings, and
humbly learn from His discipline.

verseELEVEN

Yet the LORD longs to be gracious to you; he rises to show you compassion. For the LORD is a God of justice.

ISAIAH 30:18

Has anyone ever tricked you with a Chinese finger trap? No one suspects a trap when you see a small, colorful woven bamboo cylinder with holes in each end. But put your right and left index fingers in each end of the cylinder, and then try to pull them out. You can't! The natural reaction is to pull harder to get your fingers out. But the harder you pull, the tighter the trap gets. Instead, you have to do the opposite of what naturally seems right; you have to push your fingers together to loosen the trap and get free.

Read Isaiah 30:15-22. The Israelites were God's chosen people, but they often resisted putting their confidence in the Lord. They'd count on fast horses or other nations to save them. When Israel looked elsewhere for help, however, the Lord was patient. Instead of giving up, He waited for His perfect circumstances in order to show them grace. He took action to discipline His people because He is holy and just. But He also desired to show great mercy and restore His people to a right relationship with Himself. God wanted a relationship with His people; although His discipline was needed, He showed joy in offering mercy to them because they were His people.

Our natural reaction is to do things our way. We take confidence in what we can control and earn, such as grades and money. When we try to do things our own way, like in a Chinese finger trap, we become trapped in our own insufficient abilities. While we're trapped, the Lord waits patiently to be gracious to us. Although we may receive some discipline, His ultimate blessing is our forgiveness and a restored relationship with our Creator. And that's exactly what He wants.

reflect

1. In what areas of your life do you live according to your own ways rather than waiting and trusting in the Lord?

2. How have you seen God's mercy and compassion in your life?

3. How does God's patience and desire to show you forgiveness provide an example for you in relating to others?

4. Write a short prayer to God, thanking Him for the way that He wants to show mercy to you.

BUT IN YOUR GREAT MERCY YOU DID NOT PUT AN END TO THEM OR ABANDON THEM, FOR YOU ARE A GRACIOUS AND MERCIFUL GOD.

NEHEMIAH 9:31

Have you ever played a video game in which you were only allowed to die once and then the game was over? Imagine the frustration of playing any game this way! Anything from *Mario Kart* to *World of Warcraft* allows the player to come back to life after a brief encounter with death. Of course, the player suffers some pretty big setbacks for dying, but he or she always gets to come back.

Read Nehemiah 9:26-31. Israel would sin; God would send judgment. The people would repent; God would show mercy. It was an unending cycle of Israel bouncing back and forth between rebellion against God and repentance. Nehemiah lived during a time of judgment and mercy from God. As God's judgment for their sins, the people of God were taken captive and deported to Babylon. When the Persians conquered the Babylonians, the ruler of Persia allowed the Jews to return to their homeland. In the first wave of returns, God's people rebuilt the Temple that had been destroyed by the Babylonians. Nehemiah returned during a second wave, in which he led the people of God to rebuild the city wall, providing security for the city. During this rebuilding, the people of God confessed their sins and turned back to Him. They celebrated a renewed relationship and commitment to following Him.

God allows us to experience the consequences of our sins, and He brings judgment so that we will turn back to Him. We're kinda like a video game character that gets to come back to life again and again. We suffer setbacks because of our sins and must repent from them, but God never abandons His people. His mercy is unending. We're His people, and He doesn't give up on us.

1. How does knowing that God doesn't give up on you help you to live with hope?

2. Can you think of any ways that you use God's mercy and forgiveness as an excuse to sin?

3. Are you continuing to live in a sin habit for which you casually ask forgiveness but never truly repent?

4. What's your responsibility in turning back to God when you've sinned?

VERSE THIRTEEN

HE DID IT TO DEMONSTRATE HIS JUSTICE AT THE
PRESENT TIME, SO AS TO BE JUST AND THE ONE WHO
JUSTIFIES THOSE WHO HAVE FAITH IN JESUS.
ROMANS 3:26

"Hi, Billy Mays here." TV's bearded salesman became so familiar that
he felt more like an overbearing neighbor or hyper kid brother than a
paid spokesperson. The king of "As Seen on TV" products always had
something to show us. He'd fix problems that we didn't know existed. For
example, who knew they needed a necktie with a secret pocket (iTie)? Or
more obviously, OxiClean, KaBoom!, The Gopher, Mighty Putty... wash-
ing, grabbing, gluing. You name it; Billy Mays would show you how it
worked and how you could get it for a few easy payments.

Now read Romans 3:23-26. In the Book of Romans, the Apostle Paul
laid out a clear picture of man's sin problem and God's perfect solution. He explained that God is holy, but people are all stained with sin.
Therefore, people's relationship with God is broken. God is just, so sin
has a consequence (death) and cannot go without just atonement. (The
word atone came from the phrase "at one," meaning to unify or make
amends for.) Only Christ could remove and make amends for the damage
done by people's sin. So, faith in Jesus' sacrificial death is the only way
to be made right with God. Redemption means that the price was paid.
His blood paid the price for sin, demonstrating God's perfect justice and
powerful grace.

Nothing in life is free. Even on TV. The amazing thing is that Christ has
paid the price for us. We simply have to put our trust in Him. Through
faith, we get the life-changing benefit of His power. The truth of the gospel is not an empty sales pitch. Sin is a real problem, and we all know
it. He has proven His power. He has paid the price. That's worth putting
our faith in. So act now!

1. When have you fallen for something that was too good to be true? What was it? How can you show people that the gospel is not too good to be true?

2. Identify some of the sins in your life that Christ has paid for.

3. Knowing that Christ has paid for your sins and made you new through faith in Him, write the exciting benefits of life in Christ using your own infomercial presentation. Include the problem, solution, and a call to action.

VERSE 14

Every morning the sun rises. Even if clouds cover its light, the sun still shines every day. But have you ever wondered what would happen if there were no sun? It'd be completely dark and freezing cold; plants couldn't grow and photosynthesis couldn't happen. The sun is essential for our lives, but we don't do anything to keep the sun blazing. No one on earth can take credit for the sun; it was made and set in place by God, the Creator. It was all His idea—a gift we didn't earn or work for, but we still receive its light, warmth, and energy.

Read Ephesians 2:1-9. The Apostle Paul wrote to followers of Christ at Ephesus while he was imprisoned in Rome. He wanted them to understand that they had been sinners who were not able to make themselves right before God. Sin makes salvation impossible apart from God's grace. Instead of leaving people to live hopelessly in their sin, Jesus' sacrifice made it possible to be declared righteous before God. In verse 8, Paul made it clear that God is the One who sent Christ to die, and He did so by His grace. That means God alone deserves all the credit for salvation. He took the initiative. He provided the only way. He alone provided salvation from start to finish.

We're powerless to save ourselves, but by God's grace we receive the gift of salvation through faith. Salvation in Christ is not something we can earn or ever deserve. Just as we can do nothing to earn the sun's light and power, neither can we save ourselves from sin. We bring nothing to God, and yet out of His grace alone, He offered His Son for our salvation. Through faith in Christ Jesus, we recognize that our salvation is all His doing.

REFLECT

1. What are some areas of your life that you put more faith in than Christ?

2. In what ways is it easier or more difficult to receive salvation as a gift from God rather than something you can earn?

3. How does your life reflect whether or not you have been saved by grace through faith in Christ Jesus?

That if you confess with your mouth, "Jesus is Lord," and believe in your heart that God raised him from the dead, you will be saved.

ROMANS 10:9

Have you ever seen a movie that involved a scene from NASA? Even before a launch, a team of physicists and engineers calculate the precise window of time through which the shuttle can launch properly. They consider things like Earth's rotation, the orbit of the target, fuel constraints, the sleep cycles of the crew, where the external and solid rocket boosters will be dropped, the wind, and the weather. All of these calculations give NASA a small launch window. For a launch to the International Space Station, the window is only between a certain two and a half and ten minutes a day. Talk about a small window of opportunity!

Read Romans 10:9-13. In this letter, Paul contrasted the faith of the Jews with faith in Christ. Paul indicated that the Jews' faith for salvation was based on their ability to earn righteousness by keeping the Law. This was the same Law that God gave to Moses when He made His covenant with the Israelites. Because no one is able to keep this Law perfectly, God's grace provided a way for salvation. In contrast to working for salvation by trying to live perfectly, people can receive God's grace through their faith in Christ. Faith in Christ is the only way to receive God's gracious salvation.

Sometimes it seems that people are always searching for salvation through many different avenues—religion, self-empowerment, service to others, and so on. If we look at TV or blogs, we can find a bunch of different people giving different opinions concerning salvation. Many people think that there are many windows of opportunity, and every sincere person can get through any one of them. In reality, there's only one small window. That window is Jesus, and we must put our faith in Him alone for salvation.

reflect

1. In what ways do you act as if you can earn your salvation?

2. Why can it be difficult to share with others that Jesus is the only way for salvation?

3. How does faith in Christ for salvation require you to humbly approach God?

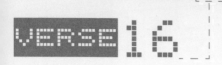
THEREFORE, IF ANYONE IS IN
CHRIST, HE IS A NEW CREATION;
THE OLD HAS GONE, THE NEW HAS COME!

2 CORINTHIANS 5:17

One of the coolest features about an iPhone or an iPod Touch is the apps. You might have other similar gadgets with apps as well. The best thing about apps is that most of them are constantly being upgraded. When the developer has worked to improve it, you simply have to tell the phone (or iPod) to upgrade and voila—the app is improved! Maps are updated. Games have new levels. New restaurants are added.

Read 2 Corinthians 5:17-20. Paul sent several letters to the church at Corinth and also visited them as he tried to correct some of their problems. You see, Corinth was as immoral a place as you could find, and some of this immorality was seeping into the Corinthian church. In the midst of this, Paul was trying to help a group of relatively young believers know what it meant to live as Christ-followers and not followers of the world. In verse 17, Paul clued the Corinthians in to a pretty important truth. He wanted them to know that when they began to follow Christ, God made them new persons. The immorality of their past was not to be a part of them anymore. They were new people!

As followers of Christ, God has changed our lives and made us new people. Sometimes we think this means that God's presence in our lives works kind of like an upgrade: God just swoops in and makes us better, similar to an app upgrade. But that's not it at all. When Christ enters into our lives, our old self literally dies. And in its place is a new self, a new creation. God's grace doesn't upgrade our lives. It radically transforms us into something new so that we reflect Him as we become more like Him.

1. In your own words, describe what you think Paul meant when he wrote "the old has gone"? Why is this so important?

2. If you're honest, what parts of your old self still hang around?

3. Write or say a prayer to God. Tell Him you believe that He has put your old life to death. Ask Him right now for the strength today to once and for all turn from the ways of the "dead you" and walk in the new way of the "living you."

SEVENTEEN

AND THE SECOND IS LIKE IT: "LOVE
YOUR NEIGHBOR AS YOURSELF."
MATTHEW 22:39

People love to argue about who's the greatest. It doesn't matter what the "who" is great at—it's an argument that lives in virtually every discipline. Who's the greatest baseball player: Babe Ruth, Willie Mays, or Ted Williams? What's the greatest movie of all time: *Gone with the Wind, Citizen Kane,* or *Hannah Montana: The Movie*? (OK, so no one has ever really had that argument. Just seeing if you were paying attention.) These "greatest" arguments provide us with somewhat of a "best of" list in each category—a list of the players we should all know or a list of the movies we should all watch.

Read Matthew 22:36-40. Jesus' ministry on this earth was about teaching and showing people the ways of God's Kingdom. In this passage, Jesus was conversing with the leaders of various prominent religious sects of His time. These leaders often debated which of God's commandments were of more importance than others. One of these religious guys, a Pharisee, thought He would trick Jesus by asking which commandment was more important than all the others. Jesus responded that loving God with one's whole self is the greatest, and the other greatest command is loving one's neighbor. Jesus explained that these two commandments sum up the application of the entire Law: love God, love people.

The religious leaders of the day wanted a "best of" list for God's commandments. But Jesus explained that there are really just two commandments that take care of everything. Our love for God is absolute priority. We're created for and intended to have a relationship with Him. However, Jesus also specifically noted that people are also expected to have loving relationships with others. We were created to love God but to also love others as much as we love ourselves.

1. How would your interaction with your friends suddenly change if you looked after their interests in the same way that you look after your own?

2. What keeps you from loving others as you love your self?

3. What if you committed today to act in love toward three people whom you're not normally excited about being kind to? Write down some names of people who might fit this description. Pray that God will give you the strength to follow through.

VERSE 18

All day long, people command you to do things. "Eat your breakfast." "Chew with your mouth closed." "Do your homework." "Brush your teeth." It gets old. But commands are part of our everyday lives. Soldiers follow commands because if they didn't lives could be lost. And while no one is going to die because you didn't brush your teeth (probably), it's a good command to follow. It's helpful to you and others. Why would you not follow that command?

Read John 15:9-14. In John 15:12, Jesus gave His followers a command to love each other in the same way that He loved. He was talking to the disciples, trying to get them to see that their community needed to be marked by divine love. This was one of the last commands He gave them before He was crucified. So how did Jesus love? The greatest act of love that Jesus performed was dying for the sins of the world. He gave His life in our place. That's how Jesus showed love.

The Bible says that they (non-believers) will know us (believers) by our love for each other. And that's hard, right? Some people are so... unlovable. Jesus says, "Deal with it." This love is not a feeling; emotions change all the time. This kind of love is a choice. Think back to a year ago. Do you like the same songs? Do you have the same celebrity crush? Probably not. We make a choice to love. He commands that we love each other as He loves us. He isn't suggesting it; He isn't making a casual observation. He has issued a decree on company letterhead and signed it with His own hand. Why would we *not* follow this command?

REFLECT

1. In your life, what does it look like to love others as Christ loved you?

2. How are you going to actively pursue the "unlovables" in your life?

3. Why do you think it's so hard to love others the way that Jesus did? Is it possible to do this without His help?

4. Write a prayer asking Jesus for help in loving others the way that He did.

verse**NINETEEN**

Consequently, you are no longer foreigners
and aliens, but fellow citizens with God's
people and members of God's household.

EPHESIANS 2:19

Haiti, the poorest country in the western hemisphere, was home to more than 380,000 orphans before a devastating earthquake in January 2010. To put this in perspective, Penn State boasts the second largest stadium in the United States, seating over 107,000 college football fans. Imagine that stadium filled more than three and a half times with orphaned Haitian children. CNN reported that 300 children who were in the process of being adopted by U.S. families were rushed to the U.S. following the disaster. These Haitian children were welcomed into the loving arms of U.S. families, tearing down the boundaries that had kept them apart.

Read Ephesians 2:18-22. Because of Christ's work on the cross, Gentiles (non-Jews) who were not part of God's covenant people by birth were brought into His family and made citizens of His Kingdom. Paul said the common ground for all believers (Jews and Gentiles) was found in the truth Jesus taught in Scripture: they were all adopted by the same Father, and there were no boundaries between God's people. Together, not only were *all* of God's people made family, but they were also the home of God's Spirit. He lived inside of them.

Truth be told, we had as much to do with deserving God's love as we had to do with when and where we were born. We had nothing to do with it! It's only by God's grace that He has chosen to love us. He has rescued us and adopted us into His family through our faith in His only begotten Son. Knowing this truth, we must also see all of God's people without prejudice. Like the Jews and Gentiles, there are no boundaries between God's people. His message is for all people, and our heavenly family has no boundaries.

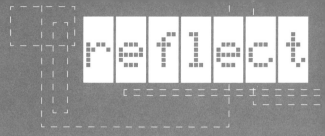

reflect

1. In your own words, write definitions as completely as possible for the words *citizenship* and *adoption*.

2. Describe the life-changing benefits of being adopted spiritually and made a citizen of God's Kingdom instead of being far off and hopelessly separated from Him as you once were.

3. How does knowing that God adopts people into His family without limitations on their race, nationality, gender, or past affect how you view other people?

4. Write a prayer of thanks in response to the fact that God's Spirit is always with you no matter what life brings, good or bad.

38

IN FACT, THOUGH BY THIS TIME YOU
OUGHT TO BE TEACHERS, YOU NEED
SOMEONE TO TEACH YOU THE ELEMENTARY
TRUTHS OF GOD'S WORD ALL OVER AGAIN.
YOU NEED MILK, NOT SOLID FOOD!

HEBREWS 5:12

If you're reading this, then at some point you learned the alphabet. It's pretty basic knowledge that no one gets too far in school without learning. What do you think would happen if you learned the alphabet backward and forward and then stopped learning? What would happen if you never learned how the letters work together for reading and writing? You never grow out of using the alphabet, but if you don't know what to do with it, it's not much good.

Read Hebrews 5:11-14. Hebrews was written mostly as an encouragement for its readers to be faithful in living for Christ. The audience was likely experiencing persecution, and the difficulties of this struggle made some of them lazy in their faith. The author of Hebrews was frustrated with followers of Christ who didn't want to mature in their faith. When they should have been in a place to teach new believers about faith, they instead preferred to sit back and be taught over and over again. Basically, they were stagnant and content to not grow spiritually. The author indicated that genuine faith reflects a desire to become mature in Christ.

God wants us to know Him. That's why He gave us His Word—to reveal Himself. Some of us have grown up going to church, hearing all the Bible stories and memorizing some verses. This knowledge is good, but it's not the goal of following Christ. God wants us to know Him and become more like Him. Our pursuit as followers of Christ is for righteousness, not just knowing some stories and verses. We must know more than just the alphabet; we must keep learning. As we grow in our faith, God's truth takes root and reflects Christ in us, showing the world that we hunger for His righteousness.

1. Is there someone in your life whom you would describe as mature in Christ? What characteristics reflect this spiritual maturity?

2. In what areas of your life do you need to grow out of living on spiritual baby food, or focusing on the basics, and move on to real food and maturity?

3. What holds you back from explaining what you believe to others? Ask God to help you overcome whatever is in the way and plant in you a deep desire to learn His way of living.

VERSE TWENTY-ONE

SUPPOSE A BROTHER OR SISTER IS WITHOUT CLOTHES AND
DAILY FOOD. IF ONE OF YOU SAYS TO HIM, "GO, I WISH YOU
WELL; KEEP WARM AND WELL FED," BUT DOES NOTHING
ABOUT HIS PHYSICAL NEEDS, WHAT GOOD IS IT?
JAMES 2:15-16

After the 2010 earthquake in Haiti (the same one that we mentioned a
couple of days ago), a video widely circulated of Anderson Cooper, a re-
porter for CNN. He had been filming violence in Haiti's streets as looters
turned against each other in efforts to get supplies. People began throw-
ing concrete blocks off of a roof, and one block hit a boy in the head.
Cooper stopped filming and pulled the boy to safety. Cooper gained much
respect for his actions. But, what if he'd just shouted well wishes from a
distance and then walked away?

Read James 2:14-17. James wrote this book to address some problems
that persecution and poverty were causing within the Church. Some people had become focused on worldly lifestyles. Selfishness had overtaken
their purpose to minister to others, and their faith had become empty
words without actions. James wrote that real faith produces action. He
said that faith that doesn't change lives is empty faith. James stated
that living out one's faith includes meeting the physical needs of others,
not just their spiritual needs. Shouting hopes of well wishes while ignoring someone who is cold or hungry doesn't reflect God's command for
justice—to care for those in need.

Let's be honest. It's easier to say, "I'll pray for you," or "I hope everything works out," or "God is in control," than to actually give our time
and resources in order to be a part of meeting needs. We can appear to
be spiritual without actually having to get our hands dirty. But that's not
what God wants. That's not following Christ. God has called us to do more
than shout spiritual words from a distance. He expects us to be His hands
and feet that touch and walk with those in need.

1. How can selfishness interfere with your ability to make sacrifices for others in need?

2. What kinds of things do you say or do knowing they'll make you look good even though you have the wrong motivation?

3. Think about two ways that you can help meet the needs of others, and write them down. They could be things such as sacrificing your allowance, giving your time, or donating items. Be creative. Now write a short plan to put those ideas into action.

VERSE 22

I ISSUE A DECREE THAT IN EVERY PART OF MY KINGDOM PEOPLE MUST FEAR AND REVERENCE THE GOD OF DANIEL. FOR HE IS THE LIVING GOD AND HE ENDURES FOR-EVER; HIS KINGDOM WILL NOT BE DESTROYED, HIS DOMINION WILL NEVER END.

DANIEL 6:26

Do you know any devoted fans? What about that girl who wears a t-shirt with her team's logo on it at least twice a week and has painted her room in team colors? Or that guy who loves *Star Trek* so much that he spends time every day looking at blogs, has a Spock costume, and makes a trip to Comic-Con every year? While their interests are different, both of these people are fans. Everyone around them knows that they're crazy about their team and show, respectively. Their lives are identified with their passions.

Read Daniel 6:19-27. Daniel was written by . . . you guessed it: Daniel! The first half of the book records the events of Daniel's life; the second half describes his prophetic visions. You probably heard the story of Daniel and the lions' den when you were younger. But the story of Daniel is actually more complex than some hungry lions. Daniel was taken captive from his home in Judah to live in a foreign land. But he remained faithful to God even when he was threatened with being thrown in the lions' den for worshiping God instead of the king. His faithfulness caused the king to declare that Daniel's God was, indeed, the true God.

People knew Daniel's God by the way he lived. Even in a foreign country, he stood out as a man of strong morals that actually drew people to the Lord. When we focus our lives' attention on God, others see Him through us. Ask yourself a question: If someone in your school were asked what your life was all about, would he or she respond with some answer about football or *Star Trek*? Or would this person say that your life draws others to God?

REFLECT

1. What are you known for?

2. Name the last thing you did that publicly identified you as a follower of Christ?

3. Do your actions draw glory to God? Or do they take away from His glory? If you don't like the answer to this question, what can you do to change?

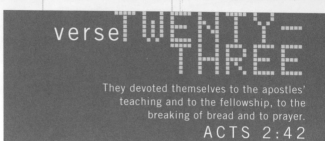

They devoted themselves to the apostles'
teaching and to the fellowship, to the
breaking of bread and to prayer.

ACTS 2:42

In the movie *The Blind Side*, the plot portrays the real-life story of Michael Oher, a first-round draft pick by the Baltimore Ravens in 2009. When Oher began attending a private school with the children of the Tuohy family, the family noticed that he was a homeless student with very few possessions or support. The family gave him food and shelter in their own home. Although his relationship with the family began with his sleeping on their couch over Thanksgiving break, the Tuohys ultimately adopted him into their family as an official son.

In the Book of Acts, Luke detailed the budding new Church. Read Acts 2:42-47. In this passage, Luke gave an overview of how the believers in Jerusalem related to each other. These Christ-followers dedicated themselves to the apostles' instruction. They wanted to follow Christ fully, so they listened to His teachings. They also dedicated themselves to living life together—eating, praying, and sharing their possessions whenever necessary. They met together often, and they did so with glad, sincere hearts. They were uniquely united with one another, and their lives together reflected their praise and worship of the risen King.

The Tuohy family was joyously unselfish not only with their wealth but with their lives. They demonstrated the attitude of the Jerusalem church in their willingness to share their possessions, family, time, energy, and lives. Our society places such a high value on putting oneself first that sometimes it feels as if we're supposed to get close to God by shutting out the rest of the world. The truth is that God wants us to reflect Him in our relationships. God wants us to be in fellowship with other believers because this is a way that we grow in our faith and reflect Him to the world.

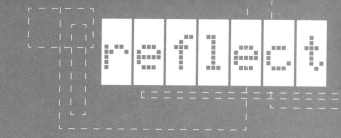
reflect

1. How do you demonstrate this kind of unity with the believers that you worship with?

2. Why are your relationships with others—particularly other believers—so important to your witness for Christ?

3. How is your love for and dedication to God's Word reflected in your life?

"WOE TO ME!" I CRIED. "I AM RUINED! FOR I AM A MAN OF UNCLEAN LIPS, AND I LIVE AMONG A PEOPLE OF UNCLEAN LIPS, AND MY EYES HAVE SEEN THE KING, THE LORD ALMIGHTY."

ISAIAH 6:5

A cell phone may seem clean enough, but through the lens of science—not so much. You get closer to more squirmy germs through your phone than from a conversation with a toilet seat! To be fair, the toilet's germs are "dirtier" than your phone's. A team of scientists from the University of California at Berkeley ranked the top five dirtiest germ traps in our daily routines. In order of least dirty to dirtiest, the winners are: light switch, toilet seat, computer keyboard, money, and number one—the kitchen sponge!

Now, after you wash off that creepy, crawly feeling and use some hand sanitizer, read Isaiah 6:1-8. Uzziah had been a great king (though not perfect), and his death was significant to his people. In contrast to seeing a dying king, an awesome vision of God as the true living King of all the earth came to Isaiah. In this vision, the prophet immediately recognized how filthy his lips were in the presence of the Lord's holy majesty. Here, the use of the word *lips* was the prophet's way of expressing his sinful heart. As a result of God's greatness and mercy, Isaiah responded to God in worship.

We often think that we're in pretty good shape, much like a cell phone or keyboard. When God reveals Himself, however, our eyes are opened to the sin in our lives. Even our best is filthy next to God's holiness. But just as He did for Isaiah, God will meet us at our point of confessed sin and make us clean. We respond to His grace with worship and a desire for Him to use us. God is worthy of our devotion and our lives. In light of who we are and who He is, we can do nothing but follow Him. So will you confess your sin, submit to His authority, and worship Him with your life?

1. Knowing that only God can make you clean, write down any "dirt" in your life that you need to confess.

2. What drives you to worship God? What part of His character influences your worship of Him? Write these things down.

3. Pray that God will overwhelm you with His holiness and His authority over your life and the entire world.

TWENTY-FIVE

BUT SAMUEL REPLIED: "DOES THE LORD DELIGHT IN BURNT OFFERINGS AND SACRIFICES AS MUCH AS IN OBEYING THE VOICE OF THE LORD? TO OBEY IS BETTER THAN SACRIFICE, AND TO HEED IS BETTER THAN THE FAT OF RAMS."
1 SAMUEL 15:22

Posers look the part. In late 2009, a couple sneaked into a state dinner at the White House, posing as invited guests. They dressed appropriately, talked correctly, and acted as if they belonged. The couple went to a lot of effort to fool a lot of people, but when security discovered the truth, it didn't matter what the couple looked like or said. After getting caught, they were kicked out because they were living a lie.

Saul was Israel's first king. God chose him, and he began his reign with full devotion to following God. His favor with God began to change when he took matters into his own hands instead of following God's commands. Read 1 Samuel 15:18-23. God had commanded Saul to destroy all of the Amalekites and all of their property. Under Saul's leadership, Israel destroyed what they considered worthless, but spared the king and the best animals. Saul disobeyed God by trying to please the people. He was only pretending to follow God. So Samuel, a prophet of God, confronted Saul. He clearly told Saul that God didn't give His favor as a result of sacrifices (religious action); He wanted complete obedience—a sacrificial life.

It's easy to be a poser, pretending to follow Christ. We can look the part and fool a lot of people by going through religious motions and saying the right things. But God sees straight through these fake appearances. It wasn't enough for Saul to go to battle with the Amalekites without fully obeying God's commands. Similarly, it's not enough for us to go to church and act like followers of Christ if we don't desire to worship and obey God with our lives. God doesn't want a performance. He wants us to obey without doubt or hesitation.

1. Which of your religious actions are easy to pass off as genuine acts of following Christ?

2. What is the difference in following God with actions and following Him with your heart?

3. In what ways are you only obeying God halfway instead of completely?

THEREFORE, I URGE YOU, BROTHERS, IN VIEW OF GOD'S MERCY, TO OFFER YOUR BODIES AS LIVING SACRIFICES, HOLY AND PLEASING TO GOD—THIS IS YOUR SPIRITUAL ACT OF WORSHIP.

ROMANS 12:1

Have you ever seen the characters at Disney theme parks? I hate to disappoint you, but that Mickey Mouse is really somebody in a costume pretending to be a life-size cartoon mouse. When that person hangs the costume in the dressing room and leaves for the night, Mickey's personality stays in the dressing room. The mannerisms of Mickey also stay there. The person inside the costume leaves and continues on with real life. In essence, you could say this person kinda lives with a split personality.

Read Romans 12:1-2. Paul had completed eleven chapters describing people's need for salvation and how God has provided the solution to their sin. In chapter 12, he began to explain how Christ's salvation affects the lives of believers in a practical, everyday sense. In verse 1, Paul referred again to the great grace of God and how, in light of this grace, believers should respond by committing their entire lives to worshiping God. This means that every part of a Christ-follower's life should be involved in worshiping God. Believers are obedient to follow God in this way when they allow Him to transform their hearts and minds.

It's easy to live with split personalities. We have a "Jesus" persona that we put on when we should (at church, camp, or Bible study). And we take it off when we don't want it (maybe at school, on dates, or in sports). In reality, we aren't worshiping just when we sing or go to a church service. Christ is supposed to affect every area of a believer's life—all of it. Nothing should be untouched by His lordship. Therefore, our lives as followers of Christ are to reflect the fact that everything we do is an act of worship to God. Jesus is not a costume that we act inside. He takes over our lives so that we continually live for Him.

REFLECT

1. Why is it difficult for you to think that you can be worshiping God when you do activities such as sports, eating, or homework?

2. What areas of your life have you not given over to Christ's lordship? What have you tried to leave unaffected by Him?

3. Write a prayer asking God to take over an area of your life that you have not yet asked Him to transform. Ask Him to transform your whole life.

> After this I looked and there before me was a great multitude that no one could count, from every nation, tribe, people and language, standing before the throne and in front of the Lamb. They were wearing white robes and were holding palm branches in their hands.
>
> ## REVELATION 7:9

Think about how many different kinds of people make up the almost 7 billion people in the world. Researchers claim that the number of ethno-linguistic people groups (groups of people identified by language, dialect, and ethnicity) is approximately 13,000. Have you ever seen one of those commercials where students in the United States are video-conferencing with students from a country on the other side of the planet? Now imagine you're sitting in a worship service on Sunday morning with a simulcast of other worship services from all 13,000 people groups around the world—all at the same time. Think about the beauty of all of those different languages, clothing styles, and cultures all worshiping the same God!

Now let's take it one final step further. Stop for a moment and let this fact sink in: All of these Christ-followers, including every believer from the beginning of history to the end, will be in heaven. With you. And you, along with them, will be praising God forever. Read Revelation 7:9-12. Remember, the Apostle John wrote Revelation while he was in prison on the Isle of Patmos. Revelation is the written account of a vision Jesus gave John about what's going to happen when Christ returns to the world. This specific vision of heaven depicted something amazing—God, the One deserving of the worship of all humankind, being worshiped by people from every group.

When we get to heaven, there will be men and women representing every color and race. There will be men and women representing Swahili, Arabic, German, Czech, Spanish, Quechua, and every other language and dialect ever spoken. All people, all tribes, all nations . . . each of them *eternally* praising God. Imagine such an amazing sight (and sound), if you can.

reflect

1. How does this picture of heaven change the way you see people who may look different than you?

2. Is personal praise to God a part of your daily life with the Lord? Why or why not?

3. Stop for a moment and write a prayer to God, a prayer of praise. Don't ask for anything; just praise God for who He is and for what He has done.

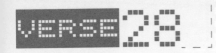

WHY, YOU DO NOT EVEN KNOW
WHAT WILL HAPPEN TOMORROW.
WHAT IS YOUR LIFE? YOU ARE A
MIST THAT APPEARS FOR A LITTLE
WHILE AND THEN VANISHES.

JAMES 4:14

Have you ever had a pet mayfly? If you did, you were probably disappointed that it didn't survive as your companion very long. The good news is that it wasn't your fault. An adult mayfly lives less than 24 hours. Yeah, that's right. Less than a day. Compared to a human life expectancy, the mayfly's life span seems pretty insignificant. But then again, think about our life expectancy compared with that of a giant sequoia that can live up to 3,200 years! Judged against that, our life span seems like that of a mayfly.

Read James 4:13-16. James addressed merchants who made plans to do business in another location to earn money. James used them as an example to illustrate that making plans with the thought that they could control the future was arrogant. He wanted them not to be fooled into thinking that anyone could plan his or her life without regard to God. They needed to remember who God is and His sovereign plan and control over everything. James wasn't encouraging his readers not to make plans. Other places in Scripture encourage preparation and consideration of the future. But he wanted his readers to continually remember that they were not in ultimate control and that their lives could change at any moment.

James gives us a good solid kick in the pants. God isn't out to destroy our lives. But remember the mayfly? Our lives are short, and we honestly don't know what will happen. We can't miss out on the things He has for us because we're arrogant in our own plans. We're here to glorify Christ and to make His name known, and we've only got a short time to do it. So let's get cracking.

1. How have you planned your life in a way that might not be in line with God's plan?

2. Do you feel God calling you to a life that frightens or excites you? What causes you to have those feelings?

3. Knowing that you are but a vapor, how does that truth change your feelings about sharing the gospel and going to the ends of the earth?

FOR BY HIM ALL THINGS WERE CREATED: THINGS IN HEAVEN AND ON EARTH, VISIBLE AND INVISIBLE, WHETHER THRONES OR POWERS OR RULERS OR AUTHORITIES; ALL THINGS WERE CREATED BY HIM AND FOR HIM.
COLOSSIANS 1:16

Zooey Deschanel wowed audiences with her stunning vocals in a duet with Will Ferrell in the 2003 comedy *Elf*. Five years later the actress made the jump from film to indie music. Zooey is the "She" and M. Ward is the "Him" in the critically acclaimed *She* & *Him* indie folk duo. Together they wrote, performed, and produced their album. She soon married indie-rock hero Ben Gibbard, firmly establishing her place in the world of indie.

Enough with that word, right? What does *indie* really mean? The heart of independent film and music is creative expression simply for the love and beauty of art. It's a "do-it-yourself because it's who you are and what you want to do" philosophy that results in unique music or movies.

With that in mind, read Colossians 1:15-16. Christ is the perfect expression of God in our world, but He's also God, the Creator of this world. He made everything. Literally. So He has ultimate authority and the power to do anything He chooses. That's what Paul meant when He called Jesus the firstborn. In many ancient cultures, the eldest son had rights to his father's property and power. Not only does Christ have rights to everything, all things were actually made for Him. All of creation was made for His glory and praise. Everything.

Christ has complete control over this world. He's independent. In control. But we're not to live in a way that reflects a "do-it-yourself because it's who you are and what you want to do" mentality. Our lives belong to Christ, and He saved us for His purposes. We will live for eternity, and to impact eternity, we must give our lives to His purposes and plans. Because in reality, it's not our life to live anyway.

1. Take a minute to write down some of the most incredible things Christ created. What is super-creative? Beautiful? Amazing?

2. How does it affect your life to know that you were created for Christ? Is it more encouraging or convicting when you consider the way you're currently living?

3. Write a prayer praising the uniqueness of Christ. Thank God that He's not under any outside influence, and thank Him for expressing Himself in ways that reveal His true character.

VERSE 30

THE LORD IS NOT SLOW IN KEEPING HIS PROMISE, AS SOME UNDERSTAND SLOWNESS. HE IS PATIENT WITH YOU, NOT WANTING ANYONE TO PERISH, BUT EVERYONE TO COME TO REPENTANCE.

2 PETER 3:9

No one likes to wait. Think about the Macy's Thanksgiving parade. Your favorite float may be Snoopy, or maybe you love the giant floating turkey. Or maybe you love the bands the most. Whatever you love, imagine standing on the street, waiting and waiting for each float to pass by. How long would you have to wait for your favorite? The parade would probably seem painfully slow from your street-level view. Now, imagine watching from a helicopter. You would be able to see almost everything! From that view, the parade wouldn't seem as slow.

Read 2 Peter 3:8-10. Christ had promised His followers that He would return, but He never told them when. They were beginning to wonder why Jesus hadn't returned yet, so Peter explained. The Lord is not confined to time. He's eternal, existing before time began. The Lord is also patient. Out of His great love, He desires to give everyone sufficient opportunity to repent and follow Him. When He returns unannounced, He'll bring judgment and uphold justice, but until then in His perfect wisdom He's patiently waiting. The Lord will return, and He's not late.

From our "street level" view of life, we don't know when Jesus will return. It can be challenging to live wondering if Jesus will actually come back for us. But we're certain He's coming because He's promised to. We can trust in His understanding and timing because He's eternal and mercifully patient. He has given us time to repent and follow Him, and He wants to give everyone else that opportunity. We wait with good reason, knowing that others will be adopted into God's family, and we participate in God's waiting by telling others about God's love for them. Any amount of waiting will be worth our while when Jesus returns in all His glory.

REFLECT

1. How are you eagerly waiting for Jesus' return? How does waiting for His sure return affect the way that you live now?

2. How does God's patience with you affect the way that you treat others?

3. How are you actively helping others to prepare for His coming by sharing the gospel with them?

So you also must be ready, because the Son of Man will come at an hour when you do not expect him.

MATTHEW 24:44

Pop quizzes. Just the mention of those unscheduled chances at failure generally invoke a wave of fear inside every student. There's no way to prepare except for the brief 30 seconds that we have to look over our notes while we take out a piece of paper as slowly as possible. In reality, preparation should have been made all along as we paid attention in class and did our homework. Then a pop quiz wouldn't be as scary since it would be a chance to reap the benefits of our hard work.

Read Matthew 24:36-44. This passage occurred at a time when Jesus was responding to His disciples' question about when the end times would come and when He would return. Jesus answered that only God the Father knows the timing. He emphasized that the point is not to figure out when He will come back but to be ready at all times. Because no one knows when He will return, Jesus warned that living without regard to His mission would be easy. But He told His disciples to continue their work of making disciples of all nations. They were to continue His mission until He returned, no matter when that time was.

Let's be honest. How often do we think about the return of Christ? The problem with our forgetfulness is that it's easy to ignore God's calling on our lives. Christ's return becomes more like a pop quiz than a final exam. We're unprepared for His return because we haven't been doing His work all along. The truth is that we don't know when He's coming back. But that's not the point. He has called us to be ready (doing His work) at all times, because He's called us to His active mission—not a life of passive waiting.

reflect

1. How does a life of actively waiting for Christ's return look different from a life of passive waiting?

2. Why is it easy to get lazy when we don't know when the end will be?

3. How often do you think about Christ coming back at the end of time? How could thinking about His return change the decisions you make today?

4. What practical action can you take to keep Christ's calling and return in your thoughts?

You made it! Cue *Superman* theme song.

Great job on sticking with your plan! Hopefully now you understand more about God's relationship with His people and how His people represent God to the world and to fellow believers. As with any relationship, your relationship with God takes work. Our prayer is that after diving into these 31 verses in different parts of God's Word, you're beginning to develop a habit of spending time in prayer and Scripture. Through this habit you will allow God's Spirit to conform you into the image of Christ more each day. If you want to know God more, His Word is the best place to go.

God is holy. We are not. Despite us, God, through His grace, made a way for us to be in a relationship with Him. We respond in adoring and thankful worship. We respond by sharing Christ to the world through our lives.

Remember these truths. They are what make us God's people. We cannot be cool enough, work hard enough, or do anything to earn His love. He loves us because we belong to Him. You're His because He chose you. Remember that as you walk through life. You're not an average person. You show Christ to the world because you're part of the people of God.

Live above average.

Linked

This book is a picture of God's people working together; a small group of writers and artists contributed to this book. Each of them is a living picture of God's relationship with His people, and they highlight this relationship through the authority of Scripture in their own unique personalities and creative voices. You may have even noticed these different personalities as you read through the book. God has created us as unique individuals, and He wants all of us to have a relationship with Him. What a great picture of the arms, toes, ears, knees, and eyes of Christ coming together to spread His Word! We hope your relationship with God is growing deeper every day and that you find as even more joy in following Him as we did in writing about it.

AUTHORS
Andy Blanks
Kennerly King
Jeremy Maxfield
Erin Moon
Jenny Riddle

EXECUTIVE EDITORS
Jeremy Maxfield
Jenny Riddle

COPY EDITOR
Lynn Groom

CONTRIBUTING EDITOR
Andy Blanks

GRAPHIC DESIGN
Brandi Etheredge
Katie Beth Shirley

ART DIRECTOR
Drew Francis

PUBLISHING ASSISTANTS
Lee Moore
Janie Walters